DARTMOOR

TED GOSLING

W.H. Bartlett, Lustleigh post office, *c.* 1920. When this photograph was taken, the post office was at the peak of its efficiency and the country postman was one of the most respected members of the community. Although this shop was a post office, which you can see by the lettering beneath the first-floor window, it was also a news agency and a stationer's. (*Roger Olver*)

DARTMOOR

TED GOSLING

Sutton Publishing Limited
Phoenix Mill · Thrupp · Stroud
Gloucestershire · GL5 2BU

First published 2001

Title page photograph: Postbridge, 1923. Of the many clapper bridges on Dartmoor, this must be the one most photographed; it is certainly the best remaining example of a pack-horse bridge on the Moor. (*Ted Gosling Collection*)

British Library Cataloguing in Publication Data
A catalogue record for this book is available from the British Library.

ISBN 0-7509-2401-2

Typeset in 10.5/13.5 Photina.
Typesetting and origination by Sutton Publishing Limited.
Printed and bound in England by J.H. Haynes & Co. Ltd, Sparkford.

> *Dedicated to my grandsons*
> *Kane and Jordan who, by stirring the dust*
> *in my mind, led me back to a land*
> *I had long forgotten.*

A familiar sight at the annual pony fairs, these Dartmoor ponies are awaiting private buyers or dealers at Ashburton, November 1989. (*Dartmoor National Park Authority*)

CONTENTS

Thomas Tyrwhitt, who was born in 1762, is best remembered for his vision for the improvement of Dartmoor. It was between 1785 and 1798 that he formed his 2,300-acre Tor Royal estate and, among other buildings, he was responsible for Swincombe Farm. The farmhouse is now derelict and the ruins of Swincombe are seen here in recent years. (*Express and Echo*)

INTRODUCTION

Dartmoor is part of the Duchy of Cornwall, and is therefore owned by the Prince of Wales. It is still called the Forest of Dartmoor, and is a wild tableland occupying the centre of Devon, the forest which may have been here having long since vanished. It is more likely that the term 'forest' signified a chase or hunting ground. It is a land of streams and rivers which drain its uplands, and they mostly start their journey to the sea from the great central morass around Cranmer Pool. Ever since the days of the Tinners, efforts have been made to utilise the Moor, and miners, various experimenters and governments have all tried in their time, but with little success. Today, the general public have discovered it as a fine place for exploring, walking and picnics. The present-day tourists no longer have the search for food and shelter that the adventurers had to face a hundred or more years ago. Even today Dartmoor has its dangers – briefly described as mist and mire. Dartmoor weather leaves much to be desired and there is much fog and rain. There are also glorious days, and when the snow caps every tor the scenery becomes Alpine in appearance.

I was first attracted to Dartmoor as a territorial soldier in the Royal Devon Yeomanry, when we used to spend regular weekends on the artillery ranges above Okehampton. Since that time I have spent many a day enjoying the wild beauty of the Moor, whether it be climbing Haytor, exploring the Golden Dagger tin mine, or just watching the cascading waters of the East Dart river. The quaint old towns and villages of Widecombe, Chagford, Lydford, Bovey Tracey, Ashburton and even Princetown all have a fascination and are still visited time and again.

In later years, as the Chairman of Devon County Amenities and Countryside Committee, I became involved in the administration and management of Devon's footpaths and footbridges, which included the vast area of Dartmoor.

There are many books on Dartmoor, but this one is different. It provides a record in photographs of its rich past. Yet again Ted Gosling has assembled a fine collection which is a worthy addition to his ever-expanding series of pictorial books covering the counties of Devon and Dorset.

Roy Chapple
former Devon County Councillor

The Weir, Lustleigh, *c.* 1920. (*Express and Echo*)

The log bridge over the River Bovey at Lustleigh Cleave, *c.* 1910. (*Express and Echo*)

'With Bill Brewer, Jan Stewer, Peter Gurney, Peter Davy, Dan'l Whiddon, Harry Hawk, Old Uncle Tom Cobley and all. Old Uncle Tom Cobley and all'. Peter Hicks, dressed as Uncle Tom Cobley and riding Tidy, his grey mare, at Yenton House, ready to leave for Widecombe Fair, *c.* 1995. The original Thomas Cobley is thought to have died in Spreyton in 1794, and the song 'Widecombe Fair' is known all over the world. (*Peter Hicks*)

The blacksmith's forge at Widecombe-in-the-Moor, *c.* 1930. Sadly, the blacksmith's forge is long gone, and today a gift shop occupies the site. However, at the time of this picture, the tap of the hammer, the glow of the fire and the smell of burnt hooves were still the order of the day. (*Olive Miners*)

Approaching Sandy Park, near Chagford, *c.* 1965. (*Express and Echo*)

1

Dartmoor Villages & Towns

Widecombe-in-the-Moor, 21 August 1956. Although much criticised as over-commercialised, Widecombe still remains dear to the hearts of all true Devonians. (*Express and Echo*)

The Dartmoor village best known by name must be Widecome-in-the-Moor; the song 'Widecombe Fair' is one of the most popular of Devon folk songs and served the Devon Regiment as a march during the Boer War. The magnificent church in Widecombe, dedicated to St Pancras, is known as the 'Cathedral of the Moor'. The church tower, with its four pinnacles holding up four crosses, is 120 feet high, and can be recognised from a distance. The site is always a favourite for tourists, and visitors come in their thousands during the season, as well as on most weekends in the winter. These two photographs of Widecombe were taken on Tuesday 21 August 1956 and, judging by the coats that the people are wearing or carrying, it must have been a day of unsettled weather, a typical English summer. In the top picture you can see that the souvenir trade was well catered for, and in the bottom picture the thatched ice-cream kiosk was attracting customers. To the right of the kiosk, in the background, can be seen the North Hall Café, which was demolished in the 1960s. (*Express and Echo*)

Seen here in the late summer of 1961, Chagford is a charming small town set in a valley on the edge of Dartmoor, surrounded by countryside. The name means gorse-ford from the dialect word chag (gorse), the ford being over the Teign, now crossed by a bridge. In 1385 Chagford became a Stannary Town, covering the north-eastern quarter of the Moor, and its standing as such brought much prosperity to the town until the end of the sixteenth century. It still remained an important market centre, and in recent years has become a favourite focal point for tourists and moorland walkers. Chagford does have one link of a more national concern: in a skirmish here during the Civil War, the Royalists lost Sidney Godolphin, who was shot dead in the porch of the Three Crowns Inn in 1643. During his life, Godolphin sat in the Long and Short Parliaments. A young poet with a slight frame, he was only thirty-two when he was killed. (*Express and Echo*)

Three Crowns Inn, Chagford, *c.* 1910, a fine old house with mullioned windows. When this picture was taken, market auctioneers would stand in the porch of the inn conducting the sale of sheep and cattle penned in the street outside. (*Roger Olver*)

Ring O' Bells Hotel, Chagford, 10 May 1958. A much smaller inn than the present one existed on the site long before the sixteenth century. The upper rooms at the front of the building were once a venue for the Stannary Courts, where matters were dealt with relating to the Stannary Parliaments, the body of people who handled the details of weighing and assaying the tin and silver from Dartmoor which would, by law, have to receive the King's stamp before being sold. The middle of the first floor was used as a holding prison for miscreants en route to Okehampton Assizes. They were kept overnight here, having been marched on foot over the Moor. At the rear, again on the first floor, were a Coroner's Court and a mortuary, and the place where post mortems were carried out in the event of any unusual deaths or suicides. In the dining-room today there is an original inn sign which formerly hung outside and was painted by a respected artist of West Country inn signs, Stanley Chew. He researched the history of the building and has depicted his findings on the sign, hence the policeman in the foreground, the coffin bearers and the grave waiting in readiness at the crossroads; macabre, but all based on authenticated historical records. (*Express and Echo*)

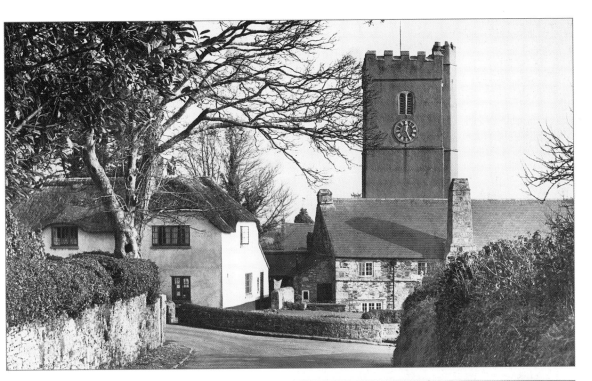

The church of St Michael, Islington, *c.* 1954. This early fourteenth-century cruciform church was enlarged in the late fifteenth century into a fully aisled plan. John Ford, the dramatist who was born in the village, was baptised here on 12 April 1586. The parish of Islington takes in Rippon Tor, Saddle Tor and Hay Tor. (*Express and Echo*)

Meavy, *c.* 1930. The venerable oak tree pictured here is believed to date from the Saxon period. Its hollow trunk is 25 feet in circumference and it is possible for people to walk through it. This oak tree is surrounded with a ring of rough-hewn stones. The cross in the foreground was set up by monks so that travellers to the Moor could stop at its foot and pray for a safe journey. This old village cross lost its shaft for over one hundred years, but was restored to its former glory in 1895. (*Ted Gosling Collection*)

The interior of the Easton Court Hotel in Chagford, *c.* 1930, when the proprietor was Mr B. Boram. The small town of Chagford, on the borders of Dartmoor, derives its name from the dialect 'chag', meaning gorse. (*Ted Gosling Collection*)

Primrose Cottage, Lustleigh, in the days when a petrol pump stood outside the building, *c.* 1936. (*Roger Olver*)

Lustleigh has changed since this 1920 postcard view. A middle-class invasion has renovated many of the old cottages, replacing working village scenes like this with cream-tea rooms and gift shops. A way of life is slowly disappearing from Dartmoor villages as a more affluent society produces weekenders, holidaymakers and retired business people who like to live the country life in comfort. The people who have always lived and laboured in these villages can no longer afford to buy or stay in the homes of their forefathers, and tend to move away to the towns. (*Roger Olver*)

A fine period picture of Peters' Stores, Lustleigh, taken before the First World War. (*Roger Olver*)

Lustleigh, 1920. With its thatched cottages surrounding the village green and church, the village is considered to be one of the prettiest in Devon. The photograph was taken at the end of an era, a time when the days of the horse reigning supreme were passing, leaving sights like this confined to the history books. (*Roger Olver*)

The parking problems, not to mention the vehicles, that exist in present-day Lustleigh are noticeably absent in this 1920 photograph. The village looks empty and deserted, a solitary dog the only sign of life. (*Roger Olver*)

The interior of St Michael's Church, Chagford. (*Ted Gosling Collection*)

Drewsteignton, *c.* 1955. The small village of Drewsteignton is on the edge of Dartmoor, not far from Fingle Bridge, one of Devon's best-known beauty spots. The pub seen on the right of the village square is the Drewe Arms, made famous by landlady Mabel Mudge. She first came to the thatched pub in 1919 and ran it single-handedly after her husband died in 1971. Aunt Mabel, as she was known, retired as landlady after seventy-five years, at the grand old age of 99. She died in a nursing home at the age of 101. The pub changed little in Mabel's time, and is much the same today. Long may the locals of Drewsteignton keep this place unaltered, in memory of a very special lady. (*Express and Echo*)

Buckland-in-the-Moor, with its thatched granite cottages, is probably Dartmoor's most photographed village. In the summer the more sheltered combes offer a luxuriant vegetation of moses, lichens, fungi and ferns but here, in this winter study taken by Dick Mitchell during February 1977, we have a charming contrast. Nearby, set on a hill, the small fifteenth-century church has the words 'MY DEAR MOTHER' inscribed on the clock face instead of numbers, and its bells play a child's hymn. This was installed by Mr Whitley, a former lord of the manor, who made it a memorial to his mother. (*Express and Echo*)

The Devil's Elbow and the Plume of Feathers at Princetown during the summer of 1989. The Plume of Feathers inn, seen on the far right of the picture, is Princetown's oldest building. It dates back to 1785, the year that the settlement of Princetown was built by Thomas Tyrwhitt, Secretary to the Prince of Wales. He gave the place its name in honour of his Patron. (*Express and Echo*)

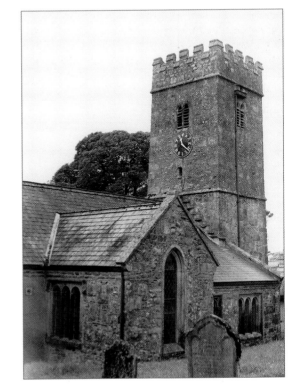

The small church of St Peter at Buckland-in-the-Moor is built of moorstone, set on a hill surrounded by delightful scenery. On its clock are written the words 'MY DEAR MOTHER' instead of numbers, and its bells chime out the hymn 'All Things Bright and Beautiful'. The rich rood-screen is one of the treasures of this beautiful church. (*Express and Echo*)

Dartmoor's most notorious building is the grim prison at Princetown, at the very heart of the Moor. The prison was built to contain French and American prisoners of the Napoleonic war. Granite for the building was quarried at Herne Hole and work commenced during the winter of 1805. The foundation stone was laid by Thomas Tyrwhitt on 20 March 1806. It became a criminal prison in 1850 and has remained so ever since. Its position made escape difficult and the forbidding granite walls gave the name of Dartmoor a sinister ring. The top picture, taken in 1992, gives a general view of Dartmoor Prison, with the television mast at Hessary Tor a thin streak in the background. The bottom picture was taken in 1993, and shows a different view of the prison. (*Express and Echo*)

Ashburton became a Stannary Town in 1305, becoming the collecting centre for tin for the south-eastern section of the Moor. Tin remained important to the town until the early seventeenth century, and even carried on in a small way into the nineteenth century. The town lay on the main road between Exeter and Plymouth, but is now by-passed. The top picture was taken in the 1950s and shows West Street, with the Rose & Crown on the corner. In the bottom picture we have East Street, taken on a wet day during March 1961. Note the Austin A30 and the MG saloon, typical cars of that period. (*Express and Echo*)

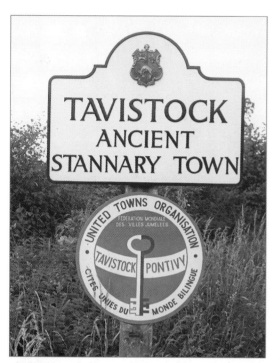

Tavistock town sign, 1964. Tavistock was designated a Stannary Town in 1281, becoming the centre for the tinners of the area to bring ingots for weighing, valuation and stamping. (*Express and Echo*)

The River Tavy at Tavistock, *c.* 1960. Tavistock derives its name from the River Tavy, on whose banks it stands. Today, the town is an important market centre for the surrounding countryside, and is well known for its Goosey Fair, which is held on the second Wednesday in October. (*Express and Echo*)

The Riverside Mill at Bovey Tracey, seen in the top picture during the 1950s, was almost always referred to as 'the old mill'. In fact, it never was a mill. It was built by a John Divett Esq. as stabling and outhouses in 1854. The mill was acquired by the Devon Guild of Craftsmen as their headquarters in 1986. The water-wheel at the mill, seen in the bottom picture, originally pumped water to a large tank at the top of the tower, which then supplied John Divett's house and the surrounding buildings, thus providing probably the first piped water supply in the town. The water-wheel was restored in 1998 and opened by Lady Peyton, but does not now perform any function. (*Express and Echo*)

This ancient flight of steps, pictured in about 1935, approaches the parish church of St Peter, St Paul and St Thomas of Canterbury at Bovey Tracey. The church is a fifteenth-century building with a fourteenth-century tower. The outer north aisle was added in 1858 and the nave arcades of Beer stone have carved capitals of unusual design. (*Express and Echo*)

Courtenay Street, Newton Abbot, *c.* 1930. Still a busy market town and a shopping centre for Dartmoor folk today, the town was the place from which the railway first pushed out to Bovey Tracey, Lustleigh and Moretonhampstead. (*Ted Gosling Collection*)

Okehampton, September 1979. Okehampton was founded by Baldwin-de-Brionne, the Norman Sheriff of Devon, before 1086. It stands to the north of the northernmost boundary of the Dartmoor National Park. At the time of this picture, one of the two main London to Cornwall roads, the A30, ran through it. This caused hazards and noise for the local people and, although a by-pass was first proposed in 1963, it was twenty-three years before work on this project commenced. (*Express and Echo*)

Old Almshouses, Moretonhampstead, *c.* 1901. Although almshouses served a useful purpose, elderly country folk lived in fear of being made to leave their cottages to live in places like this or, even worse, the workhouse. This picturesque group of granite almshouses, with the open gallery in front, was built during the reign of Charles I. Today they attract the attention of the tourists who pass through Moretonhampstead on their way to the Moor. (*Ted Gosling Collection*)

The Old Inn at Widecombe-in-the-Moor was built in the fourteenth century and sits beneath the elegant, 120-foot high granite tower of the church of St Pancras, otherwise known as the 'Cathedral of the Moor'. Although the Old Inn was devastated by fire in the 1970s, much of the original stonework and the fireplaces still remain. The building is reputed to be haunted by two ghosts, one of a man called Harry and the other a young girl who has been heard crying in an upstairs bedroom. The top picture was taken in 1901, and the bottom picture during the spring of 2000 – you can see the restaurant extension to the left of the building. (Above: *The Old Inn*; below: *Ted Gosling Collection*)

Lustleigh village, *c.* 1922. (*Roger Olver*)

Lustleigh station, *c.* 1952. The romance of steam is captured in this photograph, which conjures up those far-gone days when these graceful locomotives slipped gently along rural branch lines and the railway was an essential part of country life. (*Roger Olver*)

St Andrews Close, Ashburton, 1976. In that year the little street won the Arnold Sayers award for house design. This development, consisting of twenty-four cottages, flats and a community centre, was designed by Seagrim and Read, the Paignton architects. The award scheme, which looks for good design and careful integration with surroundings, was organised by the Devon Conservation Forum. (*Express and Echo*)

A Benedictine Abbey was established at Buckfast in about 1030, and endowed by King Canute. In 1148 it became a Cistercian monastery, and remained so until the Dissolution. It later came into the hands of Sir Thomas Dennis, who stripped the Abbey buildings and reduced them to a ruin. The present Abbey Church, pictured here in about 1957, was built by a community of French Benedictine monks. With never more than six men working, the rebuilding took twenty-five years, and the church was consecrated on 25 August 1932 by Cardinal Bourne, Archbishop of Westminster. (*Express and Echo*)

The Bovey Tracey Potteries, pictured here in the 1960s, played an important part in the prosperity of the town. Large deposits of pipe clay and potters clay occurred locally, and at one time there were sixteen kilns in operation, employing over 200 workers. At its height, it was the largest pottery in the south-west. The House of Marbles and Teign Valley Glass now occupy the site, and present-day visitors are welcome to view the old pottery building, with its listed kilns, and visit the museum which explains the history of the Bovey Potteries. (*Express and Echo*)

Lustleigh Church, *c. 1936*. The church of St John the Baptist ranges in date from the thirteenth to the sixteenth century, and is a most attractive building. The rood-screen is the great treasure of the church and bears the pomegranate badge of Catherine of Aragon. (*Roger Olver*)

Lustleigh war memorial, 1926. This war memorial was unveiled by General Alexander Godley KCB, KCMG, in 1925, when the dedication was carried out by the Bishop of Exeter. A rough granite boulder from Dartmoor, inscribed with a cross, was used in its construction, and the names of Lustleigh men on the memorial remind future generations of how much was given to secure a peaceful world. (*Roger Olver*)

2

Around the Moor

It is impossible to imagine that any Dartmoor tourist would not have sought out the clapper bridge at Postbridge. One of the most famous sites on Dartmoor, here we have a traveller's view of the old clapper bridge from the newer road bridge, *c.* 1960. (*Express and Echo*)

Bellever clapper bridge over the East Dart, on the line of the Lich Way, 1991. The name 'Lich Way' meant the route by which corpses were taken over the Moor to Lydford Church. The ruined clapper bridge at Bellever dates from the thirteenth century and is overshadowed here by the substantial nineteenth-century road bridge. The hamlet of Bellever lies a few hundred yards to the west, and the two bridges are on the road to Postbridge. (*Express and Echo*)

Grimspound, Dartmoor, *c.* 1919. Grimspound, a well-preserved Bronze Age settlement, attracts many visitors. It is easily accessible, appealing to those who take an interest in Dartmoor's past. The enclosure, some 460 feet by 360 feet, contains 24 hut circles, and the outer wall was originally 9 feet thick and over 6 feet high. This site was probably chosen by those early pastoral settlers because of its streams, its grazing and its hillside position. (*Ted Gosling Collection*)

Sheep have played an important part in the economy of Dartmoor, not only supplying the wool towns on the edge of the Moor, but also providing meat throughout the county. In this 1950s picture, a Dartmoor farmer moves his flock of Dartmoor ewes to their winter quarters near Lydford, under threatening skies. (*Express and Echo*)

Dartmoor ponies, *c*, 1935. Very much a part of the landscape and much photographed by holidaymakers, Dartmoor ponies face hardship during severe winters. Tourists today are discouraged from feeding them because of the danger of causing accidents; the mares tend to roam the roads in search of picnic cars. (*Roger Olver*)

The rugged Meldon valley on northern Dartmoor, before it was made into a reservoir. Although the North Devon Water Board met serious opposition to the Meldon site, permission to build the dam was finally given and the work was completed in 1972. The reservoir covers about 55 acres, and supplies over 5 million gallons of water a day. A car park and toilets are provided for present-day visitors, who can enjoy walks along the footpaths which encircle the reservoir. (*Express and Echo*)

Swallerton Gate sign-post, with Hound Tor in the background, 1992. Hound Tor is another favourite spot for visitors. Its rocks have become almost as well climbed as Hay Tor. Below Hound Tor are the remains of three or four farmsteads belonging to a deserted medieval village, which was first occupied during the Bronze Age. (*Express and Echo*)

Dating from the seventeenth century, the Dartmoor Inn near Princetown is pictured here on 7 February 1959. Over 1,000 feet above sea level, this old inn enjoys a sweeping moorland outlook, with Plymouth Sound visible on clear days. Nearby can be found the Merrivale Rows, double rows of stones, menhir and cairns, dating from the Bronze Age. (*Express and Echo*)

The Warren House Inn, situated beside a bleak stretch of Dartmoor road near Postbridge, prided itself on a peat fire that was never allowed to go out. The Warren Inn was the scene of a famous Dartmoor story: on a cold, snowy winter's night a guest of the inn looked inside a chest in his bedroom and was horrified to find a corpse. After a sleepless night he informed 'mine host' at breakfast of his gruesome discovery. 'Why,' said the landlord in his rich Devon accent, ''tiz only ole feyther.' For many days past the ground had been too hard to dig a grave, so 'us salted un down'.

R.J. Lugg, an accomplished artist, was commissioned by Frith's to paint Dartmoor scenes for their postcard series. This picture of the ancient clapper bridge at Wallabrook was painted during the early part of the twentieth century. (*Ted Gosling Collection*)

Fingle Bridge, *c.* 1925. The old arches of Fingle Bridge bestride the Teign in this pre-war postcard from the F. Frith & Co. series. The bridge, probably Elizabethan, is made of granite and is now the centre point of a Devon beauty spot. (*Ted Gosling Collection*)

A relic of mining days on Dartmoor is Wheal Betsy near Mary Tavy, pictured here during the winter months of 1969. Wheal Betsy was an important lead mine in the 1790s and continued to produce lead and silver during the nineteenth century. 'Wheal' is a Cornish word for mine. (*Express and Echo*)

Hound Tor, *c.* 1965. Some parts of the Moor have gathered many legends about them, and I have heard that the dramatic pile of rocks at Hound Tor are supposed to be the Wisht hounds. One of the famous old Dartmoor beliefs, the Wisht hounds were supposed to hunt over the Moor at night, jet black, breathing fire, followed by a tall, dark huntsman. They were, it was said, the spirits of children who had died unbaptised. Mere stones by day, but a ghastly pack at night, I must admit that from certain angles, with a little imagination, they do look like great dark hounds looking down at you. (*Express and Echo*)

These two parallel lines of stone, seen here in 1966, are part of the remains of the Hay Tor granite 'tramway'. Linking the quarrying of Hay Tor to Teigngrace, the tramway was almost certainly built for the new London Bridge contract which began in 1825. Demand for the granite was short-lived and by 1858 the tramway was closed for good. (*Express and Echo*)

The peat beds at the source of the Rattle brook, between Great Links Tor and Hare Tor, attracted the West of England Compressed Peat Company, who used compression to eliminate water from the peat. Work commenced in 1878, but lasted little more than two years. The appropriately named Bleak House, seen here in ruins in 1993, was once home to the manager of the peat company. (*Express and Echo*)

Drizzle Menhir, 1992. At 14 feet, this magnificent menhir is one of the tallest on Dartmoor. After falling down, it was re-erected in 1893. (*Express and Echo*)

The Path Fields, Lustleigh, *c.* 1920. (*Roger Olver*)

Dartmeet, pictured here, was and still is a popular gathering place for visitors. Families flock here during the summer months to enjoy picnics and play on the stepping-stones in the river. (*Express and Echo*)

Hay Tor, 1899. I have been told that there are around 170 tors on Dartmoor. The most visited must be Hay Tor, often condemned for its popularity, but always a firm favourite of mine – I know I am on the Moor when I see that familiar rock formation.

The Nutcracker Logan Stone above Lustleigh Cleave, *c.* 1910. This Logan Stone forms part of a group of rocks at Sharpitor, overlooking the River Bovey, and was a popular picnic spot for Lustleigh folk. The Christening Stone is the tallest rock on the right. (*Roger Olver*)

Lustleigh Cleave, 1910. Lustleigh Cleave, a beautiful wooded valley strewn with granite boulders, is one of those beauty spots which is not so popular with today's visitors to Dartmoor. At the beginning of the twentieth century, most of the tourists who came to Lustleigh arrived by train to visit the Cleave, but few people go there now compared with other parts of Dartmoor. (*Roger Olver*)

During the first half of the twentieth century, consumption, or TB, was a mighty killer. Patients were recommended to take the Dartmoor air, and the sanatorium at Hawkmoor near Bovey Tracey, pictured here on 14 August 1953, was used by people suffering from the disease. Modern drugs have virtually eradicated the disease from the UK, and Torbay Health Authority put in an application to change the site from hospital to residential use in 1988. (*Express and Echo*)

A general view of Hamilton Down, Lustleigh, *c.* 1924. (*Roger Olver*)

Here is a typical Dartmoor scene, as white clouds and shadows chase across the sky behind Longstone Hill. Although not dated, the picture appears to have been taken in mid-summer, a time when the August heathers gleam purple on the Moor and motor traffic is at its height. The pony trekkers are avoiding the traffic pressure and discovering a more relaxed way of enjoying the Moor. There are riding centres in nearly every parish, which cater for complete beginners or experienced riders. (*Express and Echo*)

This view from Combestone Tor was taken on 9 October 1958. The sweep of the hills stretches away with a variety of form and outline. Below lies Dartmeet with Badgers Holt, and the contrast between the moorland slopes and the granite rock is vividly portrayed. (*Express and Echo*)

Judges of Hastings mass-produced stereotyped postcard views of tourist areas in many towns, cities and the countryside. They were printed in a wide variety of styles. This one of Brent Tor was taken in the 1930s. (*E.S. Gosling Collection*)

You are left with a stunning sense of solitude when you view this Dartmoor picture. This granite cross, near Cadover Bridge, was one of the many used to mark moorland tracks and provide landmarks to guide travellers. (*Express and Echo*)

This fine picture of Bellever Bridge, over the East Dart, was taken on 30 January 1971. Below the bridge you can see the remains of the thirteenth-century clapper bridge with three openings. Massive granite slabs still span the eastern and western openings, but the centre stone has been displaced and no trace of it appears in the stream below. (*Express and Echo*)

One of Dartmoor's seemingly ageless antiquities is Childe's tomb near Princetown, seen here during the late summer of 1965. This restored monument is supposed to mark the site of the huntsman Childe's death. Childe of Plymstock went out hunting on Dartmoor, where he was caught out by a snow storm. The snow was deep and he had no way of escape, so he killed his horse, disembowelled him, and crept into the carcass to obtain warmth and shelter. Unfortunately, fate decreed that he should die, and we are left with the tradition that he made his will, written in blood on stones, giving all his land to whoever found him. How old this legend may be is uncertain, but it could be another of those salting fathers' tales. (*Express and Echo*)

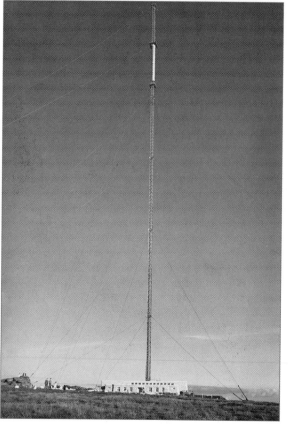

The radio and TV mast at Hessary Tor at Princetown was built in 1963 only after considerable opposition – well organised and mainly from newcomers to the Moor. After much controversy, the mast was erected and served to bring better TV reception to people over a wide area of Devon. The station building and the permanent 750-foot mast, photographed here in 1976, has now become a part of the landscape and in no way disfigures the skyline. (*Express and Echo*)

From time immemorial foot travellers over the Moor have used this little clapper bridge over the Wallabrook, pictured here in about 1910. (*Ted Gosling Collection*)

The brooding sense of Dartmoor's past is reflected in this early twentieth-century photograph showing the ridge from Rough Tor, along East Mill Tor to Yes Tor. At the present time, Yes Tor, 2,030 feet high, forms part of the huge Okehampton and Willsworthy military training area. In 1991 the Duchy of Cornwall extended a further 21-year lease to the army for training purposes. (*Ted Gosling Collection*)

The Anglers Rest at Fingle Bridge, 1970. This popular restaurant developed from a booth from which Granny Ashplant sold teas. Before that, refreshments were sold at the Old Mill, which stood on the other side of Fingle Bridge. When the Old Mill burned down, the local landowner suggested to Granny Ashplant that she should continue this service to the visitors. She commenced her business in 1897, and later bought the land on which the booth stood. Four generations on and the Ashplant family are still providing a full range of refreshments, which include delicious cream teas. Granny Ashplant would be proud that her family are continuing with a business she started over 100 years ago. (*Express and Echo*)

The Newton Abbot to Moretonhampstead railway line opened on 4 July 1866. It was 12 miles long and passed through Heathfield, Teigngrace, Bovey Tracey and Lustleigh. For nearly a century this small branch line served the local rural community, until that sad day on 2 March 1959 when a great silence fell upon the line as the axe of economy swung. During the 1920s, when this picture was taken near Lustleigh, eleven trains a day made the run along the line. (*Express and Echo*)

This 1969 picture shows an angler hoping for a catch from the River Teign at Fingle Bridge. Built over the Teign in the early seventeenth century, Fingle Bridge is a Dartmoor beauty spot much favoured by tourists during the summer season. The river flowing over the rocks and the trees lining the bank combine to make this an enchanting scene, which this photographer ably captured on camera. (*Express and Echo*)

The craggy ravine at Lustleigh Cleave, *c.* 1910. (*Roger Olver*)

'One and four halves to Chagford, please.' (*Express and Echo*)

The summer of 1963, and on 12 July that year these children were enjoying traditional fun in the shallows of Hexworthy Bridge. (*Express and Echo*)

Walkers on the Fourwinds Walk at the Upper Merrivale tin mine, 6 November 1994. The excavation of this tin mine was carried out in 1990/91 by the Dartmoor Tinworking Research Group. In the bottom picture the walkers gather to inspect the tin mine, and in the photograph to the right the blowing house can be seen. Blowing houses first made their appearance in the early fourteenth century. They were usually constructed on the bank of a stream, where the water flow would power a water-wheel operating a bellows, which would allow the layers of tin ore and charcoal to be raised to a very high temperature. The molten tin was recovered from the base of the granite furnace and ladled into granite moulds to form ingots of about 200 lb each. These were taken to one of the four Stannary Towns (Plympton, Chagford, Ashburton or Tavistock) for assay, during which process the ingot was 'coigned' (a piece cut off the corner) and checked for purity – and the inevitable 'coinage', or tax, was paid. Note the Mortar Stone on the left of the picture. (*Gordon Chapman*)

Fascinating relics of a bygone industry: the Cherrybrook Powder Mills, 1978. It was in 1845 that George Frean, a Plymouth alderman, obtained a licence for the erection of a set of mills and a magazine on the Cherrybrook estate, with gunpowder manufacture commencing in 1846. Most of the gunpowder produced would have been sold to mines and quarries on the Moor, and in their busiest years these mills employed up to 100 men. The factory closed in 1897, and some of the buildings were used as stock shelters. In the top picture are the ruins of the powder mills, and below we have the mortar that was used to test the quality of the powder by measuring the distance it would fire a cannon ball. (*Dartmoor National Park Authority*)

Deserted medieval settlements at Houndtor, Manaton. These photographs show the deserted medieval 'village' of Houndtor and an outlying settlement some 300 yards further to the north-west, with part of their associated field system. These were excavated in the 1960s by Mrs E.M. Minter. Although popularly known as a village, the larger site is really a hamlet consisting of eight houses, one shed and three corn-drying barns. The stone buildings date from the mid-thirteenth century and both sites appear to have been abandoned in the mid-fourteenth century. However, excavated evidence showed that a sequence of turf-walled buildings underlay the stone ones and that the origins of the settlement may go as far back as the seventh or eighth century AD. Indeed, the area was settled and farmed in prehistoric times, and the smaller medieval site (Houndtor 2) was built directly within a prehistoric enclosure and reused two prehistoric houses. The field pattern is also of interest, indicating development from prehistoric times to the nineteenth century AD. The thin ridge and furrow south of Houndtor 1 may relate to the last episode of ploughing activity in this area during the Napoleonic Wars. The top picture is the view from the medieval village, looking towards Hound Tor, and the bottom picture shows the corn-drying barn. (*Dartmoor National Park Authority*)

The Cleave Hotel, Lustleigh, *c.* 1930. This fifteenth-century thatched inn is delightfully situated in the heart of the picturesque village of Lustleigh. (*Roger Olver*)

A picnic party on Dartmoor, 1924. (*Ted Gosling Collection*)

The waterfall background and sunlight on the path combine to make this a striking photograph. The three horse riders are passing the area where the Devonport leat enters the Burrator reservoir, *c.* 1965. (*Express and Echo*)

The fine interior of Lustleigh Rectory, *c.* 1915. (*Roger Olver*)

Wreyland *c.* 1910. Wreyland, close to Lustleigh in South Devon, was home to Cecil Torr, who lived in this house. He was born on 11 October 1857 and moved to Wreyland in November 1914. He died on 17 December 1928. His grandfather had gone to live in Wreyland in 1837 and in this quiet place spent the last thirty years of his life. Cecil Torr was a classical scholar and a wit. He used the correspondence of his brother, father and grandfather, as well as his own observations, in his book *Small Talk at Wreyland*, which was first published in three volumes between 1916 and 1923. (*Roger Olver*)

Postbridge, 1904. The clapper bridge pictured here is the best remaining example of the pack-horse bridges of the thirteenth century; it must also be the most photographed. These bridges were crudely constructed of rough shapes of granite heaped on each other. This clapper bridge at Postbridge crosses the East Dart. (*Ted Gosling Collection*)

3

Just People

For generations of country children, the village school has played an important role; it has not only taught them the 'three Rs', but has also given them a sense of continuity as they attend the same school as their parents and grandparents. This group of happy children were pupils at the Widecombe-in-the-Moor village school, *c*. 1966, which, despite over 1,000 rural schools closing since that date, still remains open. A village that attracts young families with children is a living village: your roots always tend to lie in the place you worked and raised your children. (*Olive Miners*)

Nine community-based rangers cover Dartmoor, and while their primary duty is to help and advise visitors, they are also responsible for looking after the footpath and bridleway network on the Moor. Their many and varied jobs include erecting stiles, gates and signs; building and repairing footbridges; monitoring the state of the land and buildings belonging to the Dartmoor Authority; and clearing up litter left behind by careless tourists. They do a splendid job, and deserve much praise. Before he left for a job in Lancashire, Tom Pridmore was one of the Dartmoor rangers, and is seen in the top picture giving advice to a party from Coventry Polytechnic on a field craft expedition in September 1985. The bottom picture was also taken during September 1985, and Tom is pictured keeping watch at Hay Tor car park. (*Express and Echo*)

Richard Kerwick, the village blacksmith at Widecombe, poses with Percy Prowse, the local shopkeeper, who is sitting down on the right. The little girls are family members. (*Olive Miners*)

These men have gathered together at their local, the Old Inn, Widecombe-in-the-Moor, to celebrate winning a competition in an ancient art which has been practised for centuries. They are members of the Widecombe bell-ringing team, and the man drinking from the cup is Bill Miners. Others in this picture include Les Edworthy, Ray Norris and Frank Dowrick. (*Olive Miners*)

A profusion of flowers adds fragrance and colour to these cottage yards, pictured here during August 1970. The special pride that a gardener feels is reflected in the face of Mrs W. Rice, seen in the top picture tending the blooms at her home in New Street, Chagford. In the bottom picture, Mrs B. Morcombe, also of New Street, waters here colourful garden, truly a labour of love. (*Express and Echo*)

Period flavour is especially evident in this carefully arranged wedding group, captured for posterity on 16 May 1929. The photograph was taken in the platt at the rear of the New Inn (now the Elephant's Nest pub) at Horndon, near Mary Tavy. The wedding joined two well-known Dartmoor families. The bridegroom, Frederick Sargent, lived at Mary Tavy and came from a mining family who left Cornwall in 1583. He had worked at the Wheal Friendship tin mine and also went to Africa to work at the Broomassie mines. The bride, Jenny Doidge, was the daughter of the landlord at the New Inn, Horndon. Her father also ran a farm and his pub was the farmhouse. Cloche hats, worn by the ladies, had a brief life, and this picture is typical of the 'gay twenties'. (*Bill Sargent*)

Olive Miners enjoys a drink and a natter in the Old Inn at Widecombe, 1990. Olive, in the centre, is with her nephew and niece, who were on holiday from Australia. (*Olive Miners*)

Attractive Maria Kusma looks well wrapped-up to keep out the cold at Christmas time 1999. (*Maria Kusma*)

Sisters Daisy, Heather, Cathy, Winnie, Dorothy and Joyce Miners photographed with friends at a Widecombe-in-the-Moor gathering in the 1960s. (*Olive Miners*)

Pupils of the Chagford Primary School get to grips with a medieval sword from the Sealed Knot, who made a visit to the school in 1993. (*Express and Echo*)

Mr Alex Morris with the old water-wheel at the Iron Mills at Dunsford, 1988. (*Express and Echo*)

Some of the fifty-two volunteers who helped to clean up Okehampton's rivers, *c.* 1990. The campaign was organised by Ian Brooker, of the Dartmoor National Park Authority, and the STOC group. (*Express and Echo*)

The 'four Bills' outside the Rugglestone Inn at Widecombe-in-the-Moor, c. 1960. Left to right: Bill Baty, son Bill Baty, grandson Bill Baty, and Bill Miners. (*Olive Miners*)

Although this group photograph of Okehampton ladies was certainly posed for the camera, it is still a good record of social history. Unfortunately, no details of the occasion or the subject are known. Any additional information would be welcome. (*Express and Echo*)

During the 1991 census, Susan Martin was responsible for delivering the census forms to 125 homes in the Dartmoor Forest area. Enumerators throughout the country used many different ways to deliver the forms, but on Dartmoor a horse was practically a necessity. In the top picture, she is seen on her trusty steed Merry, delivering a census form to Eve Hearn of Postbridge. In the bottom picture, Susan delivers a form to one of the more unusual dwellings in the Postbridge area. (*Express and Echo*)

A Dartmoor farmer homeward bound, *c.* 1955. The pictorial quality of this fine photograph is proof that the photographer had the ability to see a picture and take it when the light was right. (*Express and Echo*)

During the past sixty years, more changes have taken place in farming than in the previous two hundred. A way of life is disintegrating and, sadly, times are hard for many of Devon's hard-working farmers. But here in Chagford Market, back in November 1991, all was not doom. Market Day was the time to relax, meet people, exchange news, and hear farmers talk about the price of sheep and cattle. (*Express and Echo*)

Enjoying the summer sunshine during July 1987, at Chagford's Jubilee playing field, are that year's carnival royalty. Left to right: 'Princess' Sally Coldridge, page Adam Stock, Chagford Carnival Queen Samantha Roskilly and 'Fairy Queen' Clare Slater. Chagford Carnival Week in 1987 began on 9 August. (*Express and Echo*)

Members of the Dartmoor Rescue Group, 2 January 1989, back in Devon after working in Lockerbie. Left to right: Joyce Hedges with Star, Nicki Lyons with Dart, and Alex Lyons with Scruff. (*Express and Echo*)

William Sargent and his son Frederick, gold-mill managers on the Prestea Goldfield, West Africa, *c.* 1925. In common with hundreds of other 'hard-rock' miners, they sought their fortunes further afield after the closure of many mines on Dartmoor and in Cornwall. Before they left for Africa they worked at Wheal Friendship. (*Bill Sargent*)

Paul Ridler and David Sexton pause to check co-ordinates during a Dartmoor walk, spring 1989. (*Express and Echo*)

With his pitch in the shadow of Hound Tor on Dartmoor, what better name could mobile-café owner Alan Smith call his converted Bedford van than 'Hound of the Basket Meals'? Alan (standing to the right, holding a bottle of champagne on his opening day) has spent the past twelve years serving quality food and drinks to the tourists, and the 800 or so regulars who visit the site. The classic title has caused such a stir that members of a Sherlock Holmes Society use his van as a base for their visits to Hound Tor, the inspiration for Sir Arthur Conan Doyle's Holmes adventure. (*Alan Smith*)

Dartmoor Guide Mike Perriam (second from right) at Cramber Pool, with walkers on a Princetown walk, 13 February 1994. (*Gordon Chapman*)

4

The Visitors

In the years after the First World War an increasing number of visitors started to take an interest in Dartmoor. Walking became a popular pursuit, combining exercise with education and attracting many people. The family seen here during the summer of 1930 are seeking out the ancient tracks across the Moor. (*Ted Gosling Collection*)

Before the internal combustion engine made its appearance, the horse was supreme, and this was the way that holidaymakers visited Dartmoor. This family, who were on holiday, are pictured leaving Ilfracombe for a day trip to the Moor on 23 May 1908. The coachman has obviously taken great care for the trip; horses are well groomed, and the brass work and the vehicle are polished like a mirror. (*Ted Gosling Collection*)

Coach proprietors were not slow to realise the growing interest in Dartmoor from visitors staying in seaside towns such as Torquay. Seen here in about 1905 is one of Messrs Grists' Dartmoor coaching excursions from Torquay. The Grist family were much involved in this mode of transport. John Grist and his son were postmasters in Grafton Mews. William Grist and Sons were postmasters who operated from Lisburne Square. (*Ted Gosling Collection*)

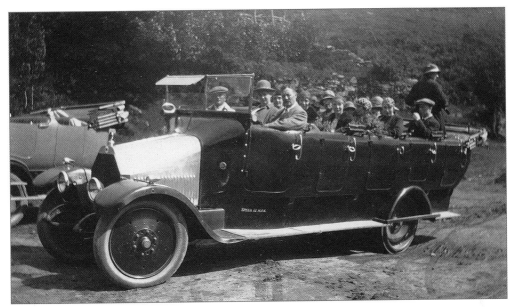

One of the most revolutionary changes after the First World War was the coming of the motor bus – which was then known as a charabanc. Here a party of tourists visits a Dartmoor beauty spot. In such photographs, the hood on the vehicle always seems to be down; was this to help the photographer, or did the sun always shine then? Perhaps our grandparents were so hardy that they were impervious to the weather. (*Ted Gosling Collection*)

During the period between the two World Wars, coach trips to Dartmoor's beauty spots became firmly established. In this picture, taken during the summer of 1932, well-known East Devon businessman Mr C.C. Gould (on the far right) poses with family members and friends for a memento of his day on the Moor. The charabanc driver, Jack Spurway, is the second man to the left. (*Ted Gosling Collection*)

After the First World War, a revolution took place in transport, with local bus services expanding rapidly. The beauty spots of Dartmoor became well served, with firms like Greenslades of Exeter providing motor coaches to visit these places in comfort. Some of the members from St Paul's, Exeter, are seen here on a parish outing to Dartmoor during the 1920s. The passengers are wearing a variety of hats. I wonder – did they all stay on when the driver got his charabanc up to 20 miles an hour, or was it a case of numerous pit-stops to retrieve lost headgear? (*Express and Echo*)

The rugged beauty of open moorland and sheltered river valleys has attracted generations of visitors to Dartmoor. The group pictured here, sitting on the clapper bridge at Dartmeet dressed in the typical clothes of Edwardian England, are not quite in the style of today's ramblers, but you can see by the expressions on their faces that they were enjoying themselves as much as we do. (*Express and Echo*)

By the 1930s, means of transport were becoming more varied and faster, and more extensive bus routes brought the open moorland of Dartmoor closer to people wanting to enjoy a day away from the beach. Motor coach operators throughout the West Country provided inexpensive outings for tourists and locals alike. One of the most pleasurable features of these trips was the stop made for a picnic and a photo call. These stops were usually at a Dartmoor beauty spot, and allowed passengers enough time to explore. In this photograph, taken during the summer of 1930, a private party from East Devon has made the trip in one of the new Parlour De Luxe coaches, and has gathered together for this group photograph. The coach driver is the second man on the left. (*Ted Gosling Collection*)

We know neither the identity of this charming young lady nor the date of the photograph, but judging by the clothes of the children and the typical Edwardian attire worn by the young cyclist, it was most certainly taken in the early twentieth century. The only information given in the caption written on the back of this picture is that the occasion was a cycling holiday. (*Ted Gosling Collection*)

Ted Gosling is seen below on his first visit to Dartmoor, during the summer of 1932. Sitting in the middle of this group of formidable ladies, many looking like Grandma from the Giles cartoons in the *Daily Express*, he does seem to have a worried expression on his face. The ladies were members of the Seaton Gospel Hall on a day trip to Dartmoor, and the group includes Ted's aunt and grandmother. (*Ted Gosling Collection*)

The first tourists of spring arrive at Dartmeet, March 1962. The two motor coaches belong to the Devon General bus company, who operated the Grey Cars coach service for touring. This was still the great coach-touring period on the Moor, with day trips running from most of Devon's seaside resorts. Badgers Holt at Dartmeet was famous for its cream teas, and coach drivers of this era remember well the drivers' room, where the much-loved Frances served them with such delicious meals. (*Express and Echo*)

Dartmeet is the meeting place of the East and West Dart, with a clapper bridge that once carried a pack-horse track across the river. This picture was taken during the summer of 1923; two motor coaches have arrived, the passengers have disembarked, and are off to view this spectacular beauty spot. (*Ted Gosling Collection*)

Ted Gosling was born in the Devon seaside town of Seaton. From his teenage years until the present day he has loved to spend time on Dartmoor; the rugged beauty of the open moorland was, and still is, especially dear to him. Ted is pictured here with a 1946 Vauxhall 14 on a visit to the Moor in 1959. (*Ted Gosling Collection*)

Barbara Newton from Seaton, a visitor to Widecombe-in-the-Moor during the summer of 1952, stands beside the famous sign-post in Devon. Before the Second World War, this sign, which portrays 'Old Uncle Tom Cobleigh and all', won a prize of £60 as one of the best village signs in the country. (*Ted Gosling Collection*)

A fine horse-drawn coach waits outside Toms London Hotel in Okehampton, during an era when the horse was supreme, *c.* 1895. The proprietor of the London Hotel provided good post and saddle horses, with first-class accommodation for Dartmoor tourists. (*Express and Echo*)

A Sunday school trip from Seaton, 1930. These people were members of Seaton Gospel Hall, and they had made the journey to Dartmoor by charabanc. The Austin heavy 12 Baker van in the picture had brought the provisions and crockery for the picnic tea. (*Ted Gosling Collection*)

The military have trained on Dartmoor since 1873, and during the Second World War large areas were allocated for military use. This small group of soldiers, photographed in 1941, were stationed near Moretonhampstead. (*Ted Gosling Collection*)

This wintry scene on Hay Tor was taken on Christmas Sunday, 27 December 1993. The car park in the background was full of cars, and these walkers were trying to blow away their festive cobwebs. (*Express and Echo*)

The pictorial and documentary elements in this picture are superbly balanced, and the composition is excellent. This photograph of the clapper bridge at Postbridge was taken in 1963, and there is no feeling at all that the scene was staged in any way. It has life, and is part of Dartmoor's social history. (*Express and Echo*)

Holiday choice, 9 August 1963. Some like to bask, others to paddle, but whatever the choice they agreed that the Meavy Stream at Marchant's Cross on the fringe of Dartmoor was a perfect holiday spot to visit. (*Express and Echo*)

Two youngsters set about a quiet bit of tiddler catching at this picturesque spot near Postbridge on Dartmoor, during the summer of 1982. Some lucky people are born with 'an eye for a picture', with the ability to take exceptional photographs like this with ease. This photographer most certainly had that gift. (*Express and Echo*)

The area around Stepps Bridge near Dunsford is epecially lovely in spring, when nature's golden carpet of daffodils appears under trees, through the woods, and along the banks of the River Teign. These lovely stretches of flowers attract thousands of visitors, who come to enjoy the beauty of the countryside, further enhanced by this floral display. The top picture was taken during the spring of 1978 at a time when visitors could still pick flowers, and the absence of blooms is conspicuous. Now the National Trust owns much of the woodland, Devon Wildlife Trust manages the north bank, and a warden is present during the spring. The bottom picture was taken in 1993, and here the daffodils bloom in profusion owing, no doubt, to the care taken to preserve the display. (*Express and Echo*)

Seven-year-old Jordan Finnegan in the sunshine of an early spring day in March 2000, placing flowers on Jay's Grave. Kitty Jay was a workhouse girl in service at Manaton. She hanged herself in a barn after being betrayed by a man who left her pregnant without marriage. Sadly, at this time, neither Church nor community offered any mercy. Because the Church refused the last rites to a suicide, Kitty was buried at the crossroads near Hound Tor. Many people make a pilgrimage to Jay's Grave and leave flowers on it. (*Ted Gosling Collection*)

Imagine Gordon Chapman's shock on coming across these Union Cavalrymen in full uniform at South Hessory Tor while he was out walking on 20 March 1994. However, he quickly recovered and was able to take this photograph, although who the men were and what they were doing remains a mystery. (*Gordon Chapman*)

Dartmoor walkers stop to view the wheel pit of a tin mine south-west of Hay Tor, 23 January 1994. (*Gordon Chapman*)

5

Winter Months

Falls of snow on Dartmoor can be very heavy, and farms are frequently isolated. However, the snow provided a lot of fun for these local Postbridge youngsters at the beginning of 1995. (*Express and Echo*)

During February 1947 Devon experienced one of the worst winters on record. Telegraph poles were smashed like matchwood by the ferocity of the blizzards, and the woods around Dartmoor Prison, seen here on 21 February 1947, were frozen into a solid mass. (*Express and Echo*)

A wintry scene at Whiddon Down, January 1991. With a covering of 3 inches of snow, gardens have disappeared and every bush looks like a frozen fountain. Snow-covered scenes with drift formations like this are beloved by photographers, who delight in taking pictures where roof and tree, road and garden have been changed overnight by an unseen hand of miraculous cunning. (*Express and Echo*)

Heavy snow at Dunstone, 1987. (*Olive Miners*)

Widecombe-in-the-Moor is transformed after a snowfall in 1983. The village is strangely deserted, no cars or tourists. The elm tree on the left fell victim to Dutch Elm disease and had to be chopped down. (*Olive Miners*)

Dartmoor ponies can face a hard time in severe winters, but they are the product of a tough environment and have become adapted to conditions like these. (*Express and Echo*)

This picture, taken on Dartmoor during February 1947, brings to mind that popular song 'Little Lambs eat Ivy' – only it's 'icey' not ivy that our little lamb seems interested in here! (*Express and Echo*)

The picturesque thirteenth-century church perched on a 1,130-foot summit at Brent Tor took on a different appearance during the snow of December 1972. (*Express and Echo*)

A wintry scene on Hamel Down, 26 February 1995. (*Gordon Chapman*)

Hamel Down was white with snow on 26 February 1995. In the top picture, Dartmoor Guide Mike Perriam is leading the Widecombe Walk on Hamel Down. In the bottom picture, also on Hamel Down, the level beauty of the snow gives way to slush, and water stands in the furrows as cattle plod through. (*Gordon Chapman*)

Hardy walkers brave the elements in winter conditions on the Widecombe Walk, Hamel Down, 26 February 1995. (*Gordon Chapman*)

Snow gleams crystalline on the trees and ground surrounding Pixies Holt, transforming an austere winter scene into a Christmas card. (*Pixies Holt*)

Christmas 2000. Snow fell over the Christmas holiday period, attracting thousands of visitors to the Moor. The white unruffled surfaces around Hay Tor proved irresistible to the children in the top photograph, who traversed the slopes from end to end on their sledges. Kane Finnegan (centre), from Torquay, is enjoying the sport with friends. Left, snow-balling never loses its appeal, as these youngsters demonstrate. (*Melanie Finnegan*)

6

High Days & Events

The Dartmoor summer bus network was launched at Hay Tor on Friday 31 May 1996. This summer bus network provided an opportunity to visit Dartmoor in a more environmentally friendly way, and also made the National Park accessible to people who did not own cars. The Bournemouth Sinfonietta conductor, Nicolae Moldoveanu, is seen here at the launch raising his baton to conduct the bus as well as the music, against the backdrop of Hay Tor. Marina Finnamore and Andy Baker, two musicians from the Bournemouth Sinfonietta, provide the accompaniment. (*Express and Echo*)

The official opening of the Ashmoor Recreation Centre, Ashburton, 15 February 1992. Left to right: Mr Jack Glendinning, founder, Mr Barry Glendinning, Mr Alan Hitchcock, Chairman/ Governor of South Dartmoor School, Mr Dennis Bowles, Chairman, Teignbridge District Council, Mr Patrick Nicholls, MP Mr Clifford Glendinning, Mr Ian Glendinning, Director, Mrs Sylvia Russell, Chairman, Teignbridge Sports & Leisure Committee, Mr Ken Watson, Chairman, Devon County Council Education Committee. (*Express and Echo*)

The Riverside Mill Craft Centre in Bovey Tracey was the only Devon attraction to feature in the prestigious 'Come to Britain' awards in 1986. This craft centre, run by Devon Guild of Craftsmen, opened during the summer of that year. The picture shows Guild Director Mr David Leach and some of the craftspeople with the 'Come to Britain' Certificate of Merit. (*Express and Echo*)

Electricity came to Widecombe-in-the-Moor on 27 September 1962. Members of the local community attended a church service to mark the event. Coinciding as the occasion did with harvest time, the church was appropriately decorated, as the picture below shows. Just visible on the extreme right of the top picture is Anthony Beard, the 'Widecombe Wag', a well-known radio presenter and once a farmer at Widecombe. (*Olive Miners*)

Traffic during the peak holiday periods, and heavy goods vehicles all the year round, caused serious congestion in Okehampton, making the construction of the bypass necessary. The problem was where to build it: to the north of the town through good farmland, or to the south through the northern edge of the Dartmoor National Park. The process by which the final route was chosen was complicated and lengthy, until finally the southern route through part of the National Park was selected. In the top picture, a wave from Roads Minister Mr Peter Bottomley at the start of the work on the Okehampton Bypass, 17 November 1986. Below, Torridge and West Devon MP Emma Nicholson cuts a ribbon to officially open the second carriageway of the new bypass, 22 December 1988. (*Express and Echo*)

Now that's what I call a good bloom. Judges John Colling, left, and Fred Harvey, with steward Pamela Rowe, at work in the flower and vegetable tent, Chagford Show, August 1991. (*Express and Echo*)

Sheep-keeping was at one time the most lucrative part of farming, and up to the nineteenth century wool was one of the chief sources of profit for farmers. Here at Chagford Show in August 1989, it is evident that sheep still play an important part in the economy of Dartmoor. (*Express and Echo*)

Okehampton Show, 10 August 1989. Left, National Westminster girls Jo Cleary (kneeling) and Michelle Read, from the Nat West Regional Sales Office at Exeter, are busy setting up their stand to be ready for the show. The showground is shown below in the early morning sunshine, before the main crowds arrive. (*Express and Echo*)

Drewsteignton Parish Charities officially opened its new Alms Bungalows at Fox Close in June 1992. The opening ceremony was performed by Mrs Elizabeth Fox and the Chairman of the Trustees, the Rev. Charles Napier. Miss Marjorie Smith and Mrs Lilly Cox, who were the first residents of Fox Close, are seen here on the left at the opening ceremony with Mrs Fox and the Rev. Napier. (*Express and Echo*)

The Dartmoor Tourist Association celebrated twenty-one years in 1990. Jack Price, Chairman of the Association, is pictured here with other officers, together with Malcolm Wood, third from right, and Mike Weaver of the West Country Tourist Board, far right, toasting the future of the Association. Mr Wood, Marketing Director for British Airport Authority Hotels, was the main speaker at an open-day held by the Association at the Duchy building in Princetown. (*Express and Echo*)

Okehampton Cattle Fair, 1900. The Fair fell on the second Tuesday after 11 March and was formerly held in the main street. It was a gathering for the buying and selling of livestock, a necessity of life for local farmers. It also gave them time for a chat about how bad things were. The smart, upright man with the top hat and stick, strolling down the street at the right-hand bottom of this picture, is John Ward Spear. He represented Tavistock in Parliament as a Unionist from 1900 to 1906. (*Express and Echo*)

In 1935 George V had reigned for twenty-five years. The jubilee celebrations held throughout the country were marked by genuine warmth of feeling. On the day of the Silver Jubilee, 6 May 1935, every street was decked out with red, white and blue bunting, school children were given jubilee mugs, and parties were held throughout the country. Here, young people from Lustleigh had gathered for their own celebrations at Lustleigh Cleave. (*Roger Olver*)

The Chief Constable of the Devon and Cornwall police force turns the key to open the new police station at Chagford, at the Pepper Pot in Chagford Square, 1986. (*Express and Echo*)

The Chairman of Devon County Council, Mr Michael McGahey OBE, unveils the plaque to open the new fire station at Chagford, 15 June 1989. Watching him is Devon's Chief Fire Officer, Neil Wallington. (*Express and Echo*)

Water Bailiff Robin Peadon and his attractive companion drink a toast to Fingle Bridge, while Anglers Rest waitress Jacquie Gillard serves lunch on the river-bed of the Teign. This picture was taken during early September 1989 when, following a long drought, the river water no longer flowed through the centre span of the bridge. Over the years this old bridge must have witnessed many strange things, but this mid-stream lunch beats the lot: and, with the food coming from the Anglers Rest, I know that they must have enjoyed it. (*Express and Echo*)

Expensive though electricity might be, it is a blessing, bringing as it does light and heat at the flick of a switch. Electricity took a long time to arrive at Widecombe-in-the-Moor, and here we see St Pancras Church lit up for the first time, on 27 September 1962. (*Olive Miners*)

Early this century the drifting of Dartmoor ponies for counting, culling and selling was one of the important events in the calendar of the hill farmer. It still remains a busy time and here, in a photograph taken on an October morning during recent years, three different modes of transport can be seen, all of which were used to drive the ponies. (*Express and Echo*)

Some of the villagers of Belstone take part in a mass protest against a proposed plan to use the Barton Guest House as a residential home for six former psychiatric hospital patients, 3 February 1982. Despite the protest, the Dartmoor National Park Committee granted planning approval. However, much to the relief of the inhabitants of this, one of the last remaining true Dartmoor villages, it fell through. The proposed plan had depended on the sale of the Barton Guest House by its owners to a Mr and Mrs Parsons, who wanted to establish the home. The sale never went ahead, and the property remained a guest house. (*Express and Echo*)

Prisoners on the roof of Dartmoor Prison on 9 April 1990, the second day of a protest against the harsh conditions, which included the much-hated 'slopping out'. (*Express and Echo*)

Hundreds of folk enthusiasts were at South Zeal, near Okehampton, for the 14th Dartmoor Folk Festival, held during August 1991. This event was revived by the late Bob Cann, who received the BEM for his services to folk music. Entertainment at the festival was provided by many artists, with several groups of Morris Men and dance troupes present, including the Plymouth Maids, seen here in the top picture, and the Heather and Gorse Clog Dancers, tripping away below. (*Express and Echo*)

Adventure River, a Bristol production, was screened on BBC1 on Tuesday 7 September 1971. In the film, pupils from Ashburton and Buckfastleigh County Secondary Schools explore the River Dart. Here they are seen after wading across the river. Left to right: Andrew Pedrick, Caroline Tooze, Kerrie Jones and John Earle, the leader of the party. (*Express and Echo*)

Many visitors to Dartmoor are finding that a pony-trekking holiday is a good way of getting away from it all. Riding centres provide excellent facilities, some with accommodation, and more and more people are discovering that, once away from the much-visited tourist traps, the Moor has a solitude and grandeur reminiscent of a time long since gone. These riders were caught on film on 27 April 1984. (*Express and Echo*)

Widecombe-in-the-Moor Annual Fair takes place on the second Tuesday in September, and is one of the most well-known occasions in the West Country. The main events of the day are held in the Fair Field opposite the village school, where activities take place such as show jumping, dry walling, thatching, vintage tractors, dog shows, classes for Dartmoor ponies and breeds of sheep, sheep-shearing demonstrations, parades of hounds and much, much more. There are also stalls of country crafts and various exhibitions. In the top picture, *c.* 1965, we have the parade of the South Devon hounds in the Fair Field, and in the bottom photograph, taken at the same time, three local ladies stop for a chat in the car park. (*Olive Miners*)

A handshake to celebrate the restoration of the cross at South Zeal, January 1990. The Dartmoor National Park works team had rebuilt the plinth of the cross and repointed the wall around the chapel yard as part of an enhancement scheme. Left to right: Eric Blatchford, Principal Construction Officer for Dartmoor National Park; Alfred Osborne, churchwarden; and William Cann, Devon County Councillor. William Cann lives in the parish and is now Chairman of the Dartmoor National Park Authority. (*Express and Echo*)

One of the most photographed sights in the West Country must be 'Uncle Tom Cobley' who, on Widecombe Fair day, rides around the village on his old grey mare. Here, in 1996, we have Peter Hicks astride Tidy. Peter took on the role of Uncle Tom Cobley, and acted the part for some ten years. (*Peter Hicks*)

7

Pixies Holt

Pixies Holt Residential Centre, pictured here in about 1998, is a former guest house, situated in the small Dartmoor hamlet of Dartmeet, that has been used as a residential centre since 1969. It accommodates thirty-five people, including staff, in a range of small rooms.

The Dartmoor Centre seeks to support schools and community education groups in a range of outdoor and environmental activities based in the Dartmoor National Park. It is also an ideal venue for staff-development opportunities and adult-education programmes. Group activities include kick-start sessions, rock climbing and abseiling, moorland exploration, caving, orienteering, problem solving, 'Earth, Rock and Water', river studies on the local rivers, pony trekking, water sports and much more.

The Centre's dedicated staff have considerable knowledge of the local area, its communities, places of interest and local people, and again and again the most successful visits are found to be the ones where they can pool these resources with the knowledge, skills and interests brought by the visitors. (*Pixies Holt*)

This picture was taken during the spring of 1969, the year the Centre opened: the girls are receiving instruction in outdoor activities, and appear to be enjoying themselves. (*Express and Echo*)

A good sense of balance required here, 8 February 1971. (*Express and Echo*)

One of my favourite photographs – a group of children from Pixies Holt gather on Postbridge for this reminder of a happy holiday, *c.* 1998. (*Pixies Holt*)

These children are involved in a team-building game, helping to bring individuals together in working groups. (*Pixies Holt*)

Caving takes place in two locations, Pridhams Leigh and Bakers Pit. The instructors provided by the Dartmoor Centre are fully qualified in this physically and mentally challenging activity. (*Pixies Holt*)

Dartmoor is ideal for exploration, and these young ladies appear to be enjoying themselves digging about in a moorland pool. (*Pixies Holt*)

Rock climbing and abseiling are popular activities, as well as being mentally challenging. They also contribute to the 'outdoor and adventurous activity' section of the National Curriculum for physical education. Here, children are receiving instruction on a programme which progresses from bouldering to a number of climbs and abseils. (*Pixies Holt*)

Splashing about in water appears to be the order of play in this photograph, *c.* 1998. (*Pixies Holt*)

Serious concentration can be seen on the faces of these young people, who are on the grounds' orienteering session. (*Pixies Holt*)

8

Ten Tors

Cannon firing at the start of the Ten Tors, 1976. (*Dartmoor National Park Authority*)

HISTORY OF TEN TORS

The history of Ten Tors is one of gradual evolution, but its original aims and objectives have been faithfully adhered to.

The idea of a youth expedition on Dartmoor arose in conversation between three Army officers who were camped during an exercise for the trainees near Sittaford Tor. It was September 1959, and the three officers were Lieutenant Colonel Gregory, Major Parker and Captain Joyner. All were serving with the Junior Leaders Regiment, Royal Corps of Signals which was based at Denbury Camp near Newton Abbot. Over their evening meal on the Moor they talked about the superb challenge that the wild moorland presented to their young soldiers. Since youth in general was heavily criticised at that time, they could see the benefit in allowing other youngsters to enjoy a similar experience.

In those days there were few opportunities for adventure training. The Outward Bound Trust provided specialist courses, as it still does, but few schoolchildren or young employees were able to participate in activities 'in the wild'. Ten Tors did much in this respect to meet the needs of the services and of youth organisations across the south-west.

The first Ten Tors was held in September 1960. It was a mild success with 203 young people participating. It was repeated in the following years at the Whit Bank Holiday Weekend, and its popularity grew rapidly. There obviously had to be a limit to the number of participants that the organisation and the Moor itself could take, and in 1965 this was set at 2,000. However, in the mid-70s the number allowed to enter began to creep up again, and in 1980 a record 2,670 participated. Local farmers had already been complaining that the event was becoming too big, and so with the agreement of all concerned a new limit of 2,400 was then set. Since that time the number of participants each year has remained very close to the agreed limit.

For the first expedition in 1960 teams (or 'patrols' as they were called for the first fifteen expeditions) were ten strong, but they were reduced for the second expedition to the more manageable size of six. In 1960 there were ten manned checkpoints only, and they could be visited in any order: the distance was described as 'about 50 miles' although the shortest possible route was nearer 55! For the 1961 expedition 35 mile routes were added, and for 1962 a long distance route of 60 miles. From 1965 any element of route choice was removed, and teams had to walk the route specified on their route card.

From 1960 to 1967 the teams assembled at Denbury Camp on Friday and on Saturday morning were taken by coach to Haytor for the start at 7 a.m. The expedition finished at 7 p.m. on Sunday. In 1960 the finish was at Denbury Camp, but in 1961 it was moved to Hexworthy and from 1962 to Willsworthy Camp. From both these last locations finishers were taken by coach back to Denbury. In 1968 Denbury Camp closed, and Okehampton Camp was chosen not only as the new assembly point but also as the start for the expedition. The finish that year remained at Willsworthy, but in 1969 this too was switched to Okehampton. With the start and finish now in one place, control was eased and the service to spectators improved. However, the use of Okehampton did present one large problem. The north moor is high and very exposed, and it is not easy to walk. Since all teams would now be required to cross this area on both the outward and return journeys, the expedition was considered to have been made much harder. Moreover, in the later stages when teams were tiring and darkness was approaching they would be in the most difficult area for possible rescue. For safety reasons, therefore, the duration of the expedition was reduced by 2 hours (finishing at 5 p.m.), and the medium and long-distance routes were shortened to 45 and 55 miles respectively.

From 1961 girls of all ages (14 to 19) were restricted to 35 miles, and until 1967 they had to sleep overnight at a fixed camp prepared for them first at Rundlestone and later at Holming Beam. From 1975, however, there was a gradual movement towards equality of the sexes largely owing to the demands of organisations that had traditionally entered girls' teams. In 1974 girls were for the first time given the option of using their own tents at Holming Beam, and in 1975 the girls' fixed camp was abolished. All girls' teams now carried their own tentage and, like the boys, camped at tors along their route. 1975 also saw the first girls' team tackling a 45-mile route and the following year the first doing 55 miles. In 1984 mixed teams were permitted for the first time: the concession was restricted that year to 55-mile teams, and there had to be an even split between males and females. Over the next three years, though, the principle was extended, and in 1988 complete equality was achieved as unisex teams of any composition were permitted over all ages and distances.

In 1977, Jubilee Year, a one-day special event for handicapped youngsters was introduced. This instantly proved popular and successful. Today well over 200 individuals participate, and the finish scenes are always highly emotional. In 1996 the event was renamed the Jubilee Challenge.

From 1960 to 1967 Ten Tors was organised by the Junior Leaders Regiment, Royal Corps of Signals. From 1968 to 1985 responsibility lay with South-west District which organised the event from its headquarters first at Sherford Camp, Taunton, and from 1978 at Bulford Camp near Salisbury. In 1986 43 (Wessex) Brigade assumed responsibility. Its headquarters was then at Wyvern Barracks, Exeter, but in 1999 this too moved to Bulford Camp. Assistance in staging the event is given by all three services together with civilian organisations such as the Dartmoor Rescue Group.

Although the Ten Tors Policy Committee has been keen always to maintain the traditional atmosphere of the event, its participants today are far better equipped than their predecessors of the '60s, and most are better prepared. Gone are the days when groups of youngsters set out on a Bank Holiday Weekend hike in top hats, jeans and inappropriate footwear. The intervening years have seen a blossoming of outdoor activities and a growing consciousness of the need to treat wilderness areas with respect. Ten Tors experienced bad weather in 1967 (still the worst two days in its history) and again in 1973, 1981, 1986 and 1993. After each storm-battered event the safety rules, especially those regarding dress and equipment, were further refined. Since the mid-70s kit scrutineering has been an important feature of the event: the dress and equipment of every person participating is inspected beforehand, and spot checks are conducted during the expedition. In 1996 Ten Tors experienced the worst single day's weather in its history and on Sunday afternoon the expedition was abandoned. A thorough review of safety procedures followed, but significantly no further adjustment to the rules regarding clothing and equipment was considered necessary.

The aim of Ten Tors is to present a challenge to its participants while ensuring a more than adequate safety cover. During the prior training, however, the manager who brings his team to Dartmoor is unable to call upon the same level of resources as is available during the event itself. Since 1982, therefore, it has been mandatory for managers (and recommended for trainers) to attend a special weekend on the Moor in January or February during which safety, and more recently environmental, considerations are at the forefront of all discussions.

Although challenge walks are plentiful in Britain today, Ten Tors remains unique in that it caters solely for young people. It has not been without its critics over the years, but one wonders how many of those who criticise have actually seen the event close up. The immense pride and joy (and not a little relief!) so obvious on the young participants' faces as they receive their certificates and medals are but the first rewards of an experience that will stay with them for the remainder of their lives.

Supplied by the Dartmoor National Park Authority

A Ten Tors team, Okehampton camp, 1976. (*Dartmoor National Park Authority*)

The finish line of the Ten Tors, 1976. (*Dartmoor National Park Authority*)

A team on the Ten Tors walk brave the elements at Princetown, 14 May 1994. (*Gordon Chapman*)

The Sidmouth College team completes the Ten Tors in May 2000. It was hot – very hot – and many of the teams retired exhausted and dehydrated. (*Helen Ing*)

Above: Sidmouth College team members receive their certificate and medals for completing the 35-mile Ten Tors, May 2000. Helen Ing, the only girl in the team, stands on the right and, in the photograph on the right, takes a moment to reflect on their achievements. (*Helen Ing*)

ACKNOWLEDGEMENTS

I am grateful to all those who have helped in the compilation of this book by contributing valuable information. Particular thanks must go to the Editor of the *Express and Echo* for allowing me to use pictures from the newspaper's archives, and to Chris Wright for his valuable assistance.

Roger Olver gave much help, and I am grateful for the information given to me by Elaine Lush. Olive Miners, Peter Hicks and the staff at the Old Inn at Widecombe not only allowed me to use pictures belonging to them, but also supplied useful information. Help was also given to me by the Drewe Arms, the Ring o' Bells at Chagford, the Anglers Rest at Fingle Bridge and the Cleave Hotel at Lustleigh.

My old friend Bill Sargent spoke to me about his personal knowledge of past times and allowed me to use family photographs. Gordon Chapman gave much help with loan of material, and Alan Smith of the Hound of the Basket Meals at Houndtor not only supplied me with the picture of his refreshment van, but also provided a welcome refreshment break on my many journeys to the Moor.

I am indebted to Claudia Radmore of Pixies Holt for allowing pictures of this outstanding residential centre to be used. The Dartmoor National Park Authority provided a wealth of information and I am indeed grateful to their staff for giving me permission to use archive photographs.

Thanks must go to Lyn Marshall and to Roy Chapple for his splendid introduction. I am grateful to my wife Carol for her encouragement and help, and to Simon Fletcher of Sutton Publishing.

The accuracy of the facts in this book have been checked as carefully as possible. However, original sources can contain errors, and memories fade over the years.

References include:

Dartmoor National Park Authority
Ten Tors
Dartmoor: A New Study by Crispin Gill, David & Charles, 1970
Dartmoor 365 by John Hayward, Curlew Publications, 1991
Portrait of Dartmoor by Vian Smith, Hale, 1996
A Perambulation of the Ancient and Royal Forest of Dartmoor by Samuel Rowe, 1902

BRITAIN IN OLD PHOTOGRAPHS

To order any of these titles please telephone our distributor,
Haynes Publishing on 01963 442105
For a catalogue of these and our other titles please telephone
Joanne Govier at Sutton Publishing on 01453 732423